In Search of
BUTTERFLIES and
RAINBOWS

In Search of BUTTERFLIES and RAINBOWS

Navigating My Way through Forgiveness, Acceptance and

finally, Self-Love

D. M. Lippi

In Search of Butterflies and Rainbows

Copyright © 2016 by D.M. Lippi

For information, contact D.M. Lippi,
email: **debwithgrace@gmail.com**

ISBN 10: 0692797149
ISBN 13: 9780692797143
Library of Congress Control Number: **2016919356**
D.M. Lippi, Forked River, NEW JERSEY

Printed in the United States of America

Dedication

Heartfelt gratitude to my children, Kelly and Jeff, for loving and supporting me in all my craziness. May you one day find the courage to write your own story. I am so proud to be your Mom.

To my son-in-law, John; thanks for always bailing me out, and getting me through the rough patches...oh, and taking care of the Koi!

For my grandchildren, Jack and Alexa. You are the light of my life. May you grow strong, happy and healthy with each passing day.

And to you Vitt; thanks for the butterflies and rainbows.

Acknowledgements

A special thanks to Eva, Adele and Isabella, three very different souls who have supported and encouraged me to never give up. I am humbled and blessed to be your friend.

To you, my readers and friends; thank you for everything I could ever hope to be.

Table of Contents

Introduction

When I began writing this book, it started differently. Originally, I wanted to talk about things like nutrition and stress management and all things about living a healthy lifestyle. I suppose, statistically speaking, things like weight control, diabetes, and quitting smoking could hold an interest for most. Recently graduating from the Institute of Integrative Nutrition certainly gave me a lot of avenues to consider. My meet-up group on weight issues and even the whole online dating thing might have been fun too.

With pen in hand, I kept going back to my personal life, an area that I thought would stay under wraps. Each time I began somewhere else, I was guided right back to the stories I had started so long ago. Finally, my inner guidance got the best of me, and I knew where I was headed. The outcome no longer mattered. This book took on a life of its own. It was no longer about me and my journey but a way to connect others with their stories through a common bond.

I had so many issues (my whole life) with speaking up; it just seemed natural that writing and speaking would turn into my passion. I chose these stories because they impacted my life and created an opening for me to learn and grow. These lessons became stepping-stones to help guide me to the truth of knowing and accepting myself as I am.

Perfection is a fleeting thought; it doesn't exist. Strive to be happy and grateful instead. Earth school is tough; life is sometimes tough. Find something to believe in while staying true to yourself. Speaking from my heart was so far removed from my existence that I shut down. I silenced my voice. Rather than risk being made fun of or getting hurt because I thought differently, I just kept to myself.

If that's you too, please don't do that to yourself. I missed out on so much growing up, and I don't want you to miss out too. This book is for me and for you and for your future. I hope it gives you the courage to just be yourself. Find your voice. Find your passion. Do what makes you happy, no matter how big or how small, and just live your life...you're the only one who can.

Owning our story and loving ourselves through that process is the bravest thing we'll ever do.

—Brené Brown
author, speaker

Chapter 1

Those Darn If'n Words

Ever since I was a child, I had this yearning, this burning desire to live my truth. I didn't know what that meant back then, but I always had an inkling that something wasn't right. As early as grade school, I was questioning things in my "if only" world. If only I were taller or thinner or smarter. If only I was born into a rich family…if only, if only, if only. Those if'n words can really mess you up. My saving grace, for a time, was that I always lived inside my head. Eventually, I figured out what worked for me. After all, who knows me better than I do?

Self-love is so important. How else can you shine and radiate that inner beauty to others and to the world? It starts within. (Nice words that meant nothing to me at the time.)

Although you could say that I'm a "Jersey Girl", my roots are in upstate New York, and I naturally gravitate to the mountains and lakes every chance I get. For me, there's nothing better than sitting leisurely on a beautiful mountaintop, watching butterflies dancing in the sunlight. It's always fun though, to be at the Jersey Shore, especially in the summertime. There are beautiful beaches and outdoor concerts, barbecues and bars. And the food, oh my God, it's never-ending and oh so good!

I began my eating journey at about the age of ten. Instead of being upset about it, I should have given myself a pat on the back. After all, it took quite a bit of eating to put on a whole lot of weight. Of course, the hormone thing kicking in early didn't help. Had I caught on, about the food thing I mean, I might have done things differently. I might have recognized that not much nutrition came from food in a can. Do you remember the can-can sales?

It was a family outing for us, when Mom took the whole tribe along. We easily filled two shopping carts.

I might have asked my mom what she ate during her pregnancy and before, maybe even what Grandma ate (stay tuned). I may have noticed there were no greens on my plate. But I was just a kid. In all fairness, Mom was raising five of us, mostly alone.

I often wondered why I was the only one with a weight problem. What's up with that? After all, weren't we all related? Didn't we all come from the same family? (Oh, except my baby sister, with her red hair and freckles. We kids' thought the milkman must have brought her.)

Volleyball and skating were my two favorite pastimes. I'll admit that, as a teenager, I did get obsessed with the Luke and Laura saga for a while, (you know, the *General Hospital*, soap opera thing) but I could never be classified as a couch potato. Funny though, I barely watch television today.

Some of my friends are avid TV watchers, so they keep me up-to-date on the important stuff. Gotta love social media. (Yes, that was a bit sarcastic, but don't get me started with Facebook and cell phones.)

Summers were especially difficult for me. For most girls' it meant cute dresses and two-piece swimsuits or more (or less). Not me though. I always covered up and was fearful of being recognized and called out for being different. Where did that thinking even come from? "Pretty eyes," they would say, "Such a pretty girl, if only she lost some weight."

"Deb," my mom often said, "here's some more clothes you can have; they're too big for me." God, I was twelve years old!

Geez, Ma. I do have feelings ya know. I mean, why don't you just shout it out from the rooftop? "Hey everyone, my twelve-year-old daughter weighs more than me!" At least that's what I wanted to say. I think that was about the time my mom took me to the doctor for diet pills.

Parents, please, I beg of you, if you have a child you believe is overweight, do not, I repeat, do not put him or her on diet pills or on any kind of diet for that matter. There's something else going on here, so stick with me, and together we may be able to figure it out.

What is the charm that
makes old things so sweet?

—Sarah Doudney
English novelist

Chapter 2

Nana and Gramps

My brother, Dana, was eleven months younger than I was. We loved visiting Nana on our days off from school. We took the Bergen Avenue bus from Jersey City to Bayonne to visit her. She and Gramps lived on the third floor of an old apartment building on Broadway. The hallways were long, narrow, and dark, and we were never bothered by the six flights of stairs.

Nana was always excited to see us. The first thing she'd say was "What kind of TV dinner do you want?"

Fried chicken was my favorite, all three pieces with whipped potatoes, mixed vegetables, and apple cobbler for dessert. Do you know they still make that dinner today? Only now it's Hungry-Man size.

Nana wasn't much for cooking, but it didn't matter. We set up the trays in front of the television, with our TV dinners and Kool-Aid. Her "summertime salad" was a big hit with everyone, and always a favorite of mine.

Those were the days. I adored my grandfather. Gramps did everything Nana told him to, mumbling to himself as if he wanted to say something she might not like. He was quiet; such a gentle soul, with a touch of red hair on his almost bald head. Nana was much taller than Gramps, and I never noticed until I saw the two of them together in pictures, which wasn't often. I wondered how their lives might have been different if it weren't for their arranged marriage.

It was a Sunday in June, 1966, and Dana and I were coming home from our weekend trip. As we ran up the stairs to our second-floor apartment, we pushed each other out of the way to see who could reach the top first.

Approaching the landing, we noticed our door was wide open. *That's strange, I* thought. *It was never wide open.* With backpacks in tow, Dana and I walked slowly into our large and overrated living room, complete with creaking floorboards and colorful dime-store curtains. Something was different. A stranger was sitting next to Mom on our old and tattered, deep-purple sofa.

"Where's Dad?" I asked cautiously.

To be continued…

Nana's Summertime Salad

Cover a platter with your choice of <u>lettuce.</u>

Cut up some jersey <u>tomatoes</u> and put on top of the lettuce.

Slice up hard-boiled <u>eggs</u> and put them neatly on top.

Sprinkle a can of <u>tuna</u> or salmon all over the platter.

The last step is to put small dollops of <u>mayonnaise</u> all around. You can add whatever you like, but Nana's was simple, delicious, and inexpensive.

Add a fresh glass of iced tea with lemon, and you've got a great meal. Easy peasy.

*Note: Today I've changed it up a bit with lots of mixed greens (kale, bok choy, collard greens), salmon, and avocado mayonnaise (for the paleo palette) and still use the eggs and fresh tomatoes. I also lightly toast pumpkin seeds and add them. You can do a lot with this salad and make it awesome and healthy!

There comes a time in your life when you have to choose to turn the page, write another book, or simply close it.

—Shannon Alder
inspirational author

Chapter 3

My Dad

I loved being around Dad; he was always there. Mom worked, and Dad stayed home. I'm sure it wasn't planned that way, but that's how it was. I don't ever remember them arguing. As a matter of fact, I don't recall any conversations between them, but that might have been because I was into doing the things kids do and not paying too much attention to grown-up stuff. To me, my dad looked like a young Frank Sinatra.

Every Saturday morning when I was a teenager, I woke up to the sounds of Jimmy Roselli; Nat King Cole; Al Martino; Johnny Mathis; and of course, Frankie.

Mom played that phonograph loudly. If the music didn't wake us up, the delightful aroma of bacon and eggs surely did.

"Let's go; we've got work to do," Mom would yell. Saturday was always cleaning day. "And no going out till you're done." We usually finished by midafternoon, so there was still time to hang out with our friends before it got dark.

Dad was a wonderful photographer, but he was also an alcoholic, and hanging around with Uncle Jerry, a heavy drinker himself, didn't help matters. Between the two of them, there were nine children, two boys and seven girls, and they usually took us with them to the local watering hole. It's amazing how well-behaved we were.

Larry, a robust and happy guy, was perfect, I thought, as an afternoon babysitter. (Newsflash—he was the bartender, but did a great job keeping us kids occupied with music and funny stories). "Here's some root beer and pretzels for you guys," he would say.

I wonder what would've happened if I asked for some kale chips and green tea?

Every so often, Dad picked us up from school and took us to the park. We climbed trees and played ball; all the fun things kids do. I remember a time when my baby sister waddled into the lake. None of us knew how to swim, but I ran in after her, trying to save her from drowning. "Dad," I screamed. "Help!"

He ran in right after me, grabbed Doreen, and made it safely to the grass. I guess everyone sometimes needs to make decisions in the blink of an eye. From Dad's view, I suspect he knew I could take care of myself, but my one-year-old sister certainly couldn't.

There I was, flailing around in the water yelling, "What about me?" As a seven-year old, I saw it differently. Of course, the water wasn't deep at all, and I made it out without a hitch.

Trick-or-Treat?

It was Halloween night, 1963, and Mom figured my brother Dana; my sister, Denise (Didi); and I were old enough to go trick-or-treating in the neighborhood. Even though I was the oldest, I was shy. Our bags were brimming with candy and coins when Dana suggested we try one more house. Al's candy store was on the corner, and he rented out a small apartment in the back.

As we got closer to the door, I noticed it was already opening. "He sees us," I said. "Do you have any candy, mister?" my brother asked. "Yes," the man said. "Come in and I'll get you some."

What an odd-looking man, I thought as he shuffled slowly toward a small wooden table and a bowl of candy. He reminded me of Ebenezer Scrooge from the beloved *A Christmas Carol*. As he approached us, an eerie feeling passed through me, and I knew intuitively that I shouldn't be there.

Looking up into this man's dark and unwavering eyes, I repeated my brother's question. "Do you have any candy, mister?" By the time I turned around, my brother and sister were gone. That was the night I was molested.

It all happened so fast. My siblings must have run home because Dad was there almost immediately. He kicked in the door, grabbed the man, and told me to get home. I can only guess what happened next.

The police were at my house in no time, and they asked me a few questions before Mom told me to go to my room. I wanted to stay and talk to them, but Mom and Dad wouldn't have it.

The next day I decided to go across the street to call on my friend Becca. Back then, you stood in the street and yelled for your friends to come out and play. Becca's mom came out. "She can't play with you today, Debbie, and probably not tomorrow either." Hmm…

Within a short time, we moved out of the neighborhood. We never discussed that night again.

Looking back today, I realized that the pain wasn't from what had happened, but that I didn't have a voice. My power of communication was shut down, and unbeknown to me, it would take thirty-plus years to find it.

Dad, Where Are You?

For a time, I didn't see my father. Mom said he was visiting relatives, but my mean little neighbor Eddy said he was in jail. "Where's your Dad, Debbie?" he would say in his usual sarcastic voice.

"I told you," I said, again and again. "He's at my aunt's house."

"No he's not; he's in jail." Eddie was such a troublemaker. He used to wait until my sisters or I got home from school, just so he could look under our dresses as we ran up the stairs. If I had been the confrontational type, I might have hauled off and punched him square in the nose, hoping for a bloody mess. Maybe then he'd shut up.

One day I was down the street at my aunt's babysitting. My cousin Frannie asked me for something in the china closet, and, when I opened the glass doors, a news article fell out. Of course, little inquisitive mind that I was, I read it. It seems Eddie was right. Dad was in jail, and there he was, big as life on the front page. Apparently, he got behind the wheel of the car while he was drunk. It did not end pretty. There was an old woman, and there was a death. We never talked about it.

Keep your face always toward the sunshine and the shadows will fall behind you.

—Walt Whitman

Chapter 4

There's a New Man in Town

There in the living room was my mom and a man I had never seen before. He was quite handsome, and with his mustache and stoic stance, he could have been a dead ringer for Clark Gable. Mom introduced us. "This is Lou. How would you like him to be your new dad?" *I had no words, just an awful feeling in my gut that this wouldn't be good.*

There was no warning. Dad was out, and Lou was in. I don't know what went through my brother's mind that day, but we barely spoke to each other again. Our childhood, as we knew it, was over, at least in my mind.

It didn't take long to see who ruled the roost. Lou was there, and then he was gone, and then he was back again. To outsiders, they were the perfect couple, he and Mom, but it was a different story behind closed doors. They looked great together, especially when they dressed to go out, which was often. Mom, a full-figured Marilyn Monroe type, and Lou, her debonair gentleman, always seemed to get people's attention.

Nana hated him, and she wasn't afraid to stand up to him either. Lou's controlling nature was not a force to be reckoned with, and I was always pushing his buttons. Many a night, after dinner was done and the dishes were cleaned and put away, I sat at the table, sometimes for hours. By the way, did I mention I was stubborn? Lou liked manners, I guess.

He said that I could only leave the table when I asked to be excused, and I had to address him as Dad. Nope! Wasn't happening. As far as I was concerned, I already had a father.

My brother and three sisters always gave in, and were able enjoy their evenings. I would sit there, stiff as a board, feeling the tears welling up, choking me, as if I couldn't breathe.

"Look in the mirror," he'd say as he sat it down in front of me. "Look how ugly you are when you cry. You can sit there all night and stare at yourself."

I might have been down, but my stubbornness refused to let me give in, and eventually my mom would come into the kitchen and say, "Just go to bed." If only I'd given in.

Lou was in our lives for almost five years. Eventually he went away, but not without drama. His mom, wife, and grown son showed up on our doorstep one day, and it was like seeing a movie in slow motion. I watched as he got in their car and never looked back. Thank God, it was over.

"How do you spell love?"
—Piglet
"You don't spell it, you feel it."
—Pooh

—A. A. Milne
English author, playwright

Chapter 5

Food as Friend

During those years, I spent a lot of time with what I now know as my best friend. You got it. Food, to me wasn't abusive (hold that thought till later), tasted good, and made me happy. There's so much comfort in food. When I reached the eighth grade, I was close to 150 pounds, a lot of weight on a five-foot, one-inch frame, and it certainly did nothing for my social life.

When I got to high school, I was taking diet pills almost daily, trying every new gimmick on the market (and off the market). The weight never stayed off, and, before long, I was battling the well-known yo-yo syndrome.

What did I know about healthy eating? Mom couldn't help. There were four other children to care for, and it was hard enough trying to keep a roof over our heads. Aside from her full-time job in New York, she was also a bartender in the evenings. Nana helped when she could with babysitting, money, and lots of food.

I loved when Nana came. We watched television, ate sub sandwiches, and drank lots of soda. Isn't it amazing how food can become the center of our world? I always felt good when I was eating and never gave a second thought to how I might be harming my body.

One day, when I was about fifteen, my dad showed up. He just showed up. I hadn't seen him for about five years. I had missed him terribly and would've loved for him to hug me. Instead, the first and only thing he said to me was, "Boy, you got fat." I tried to pretend it didn't bother me. He was drunk. Mom came home from work and threw him out. *If only I could find my voice*, I thought.

*The soul attracts that which it secretly harbors,
that which it loves, and also that which it fears.*

—James Allen
The Law of Attraction

Chapter 6

Strange Bedfellows

We were quite a pair, Bill and I. My cousin Carol fixed us up

on a blind date, and it turned out to be a never-ending cycle of

drive-in movies and Yago Sangria (I don't care if I never see

another kung-fu movie again). Do they even do that anymore?

I had just turned seventeen, and other than a few schoolgirl

crushes, never had a boyfriend.

They say we attract certain people into our lives, according to who we are at the time. For instance, I was in a place of low self-esteem, and, although my heart wanted something better, the universe was saying, "No, Deb, you're not there." Somewhere deep inside, I didn't feel worthy. Years would go by before I even began to understand the Law of Attraction*.

Bill and I moved in together. He was a drinker and a mean spirit. Some people get mellow when they drink. Not him. When I was nineteen, I got pregnant, right about the same time I found out he was seeing someone else. After a lot of desperate thinking and what I thought I knew of soul-searching, I chose to have an abortion. It was not my greatest moment. My mom found out; the insurance company sent the bill to her house instead of mine, but at least I didn't do the fashionable back-alley thing. That was an uncomfortable conversation. She and I never did get along, especially after Lou.

*Law of Attraction – Universal belief that like attracts like, and your thoughts are your reality. The Secret – Rhonda Byrne

You're Not Listening, Mom!

Our relationship was what I'd call nonexistent. Mom and Lou might have looked like the perfect couple, but trust me, our lives were anything but normal. On Sunday mornings, before church, Lou lined the five of us up in the master bedroom and reiterated what he'd said so many times before. Then his hand came up, raised as if he were Moses on the Mount. "Listen to me, or you know what you're going to get." How I hated those times.

One Sunday morning, when Mom and Lou came home from food shopping, they found my three sisters, Denise, Donna, and Doreen, running up and down the stairs to our second-floor apartment.

Doreen, a cute five-year old with strawberry-blond hair and freckles, trailed behind as they marched. "Tramp, tramp, tramp, you can hear the marching feet." (My sisters were always doing the silliest things, and although I was the serious one, I got a kick out of watching them "perform.")

"What are you doing, girls?" Lou said.

From the look on Didi's face, I could tell she knew they were in trouble.

"No, go right ahead and keep doing what you're doing," Lou said. "And don't stop until I tell you to."

I thought, *he's such a jerk*. They marched and sang (and not a happy tune at that point) for at least half an hour until Lou opened the door and told them they could come in the house. My mom never said a word. I know she was afraid of him; we all were.

Being well-developed by the time I was ten didn't help the situation with Lou. I guess he felt he had the right to touch me and fondle me in inappropriate ways.

Late at night, he would come into the bedroom that I shared with my younger sister. The crippling fear of his presence only allowed me to lie quietly, as if I were asleep. Over the years, I tried to speak up in my own way. Mom took it as me just making things up, which made me even more withdrawn. Since he never bothered my sisters in that way, they couldn't understand, and I became known as Debbie the storyteller.

Do I even have to mention what's wrong on so many levels here? Parents, grandparents, and caregivers, please listen to your children. It's plain and simple, and if they're exaggerating, you'll know soon enough. Don't let the fear of what might happen stop you from protecting them. Be an advocate not only for your child but for any child who can't speak up for him- or herself.

Yes, I have a soapbox too. What do you speak about on yours? So where was I...oh yeah, me and Bill.

The guilt of my decision to not go through with the pregnancy stayed with me for a long time. It never dawned on me to leave him. At the time, it was all I knew. After all, alcoholism and abuse were already a pattern in my life, and no one, not yet anyway, told me something was wrong.

As usual, I turned to food for comfort; somehow, it made me feel safe and protected. Have you ever felt that way? Bill and I married when I was twenty-two, and 5 months later, we had a daughter. There I thought, was the shining light. I had put on 60 pounds and had to leave work earlier than planned, to stay in bed and rest.

My diet consisted of southern fried chicken and cranberry sauce, hold the greens. Still, I felt content. Four years later, I found myself pregnant again. The baby never made it to full term. That was tough and my guilt from the choice I had made years ago had come back with a vengeance. Even though I carried on as if everything was perfect, I was sad, and hurt, and I felt like a phony deceiving everyone, including myself.

One day, I decided to talk to a friend about my situation. Lori was married with two children and what seemed to be a happy marriage. After we talked, she went home and told her husband everything. He forbade her to see me again. Her last words to me were "I'm sorry Deb, but Tommy feels that if I hang around with you, some of your "stuff" will rub off on me and he won't allow it." Are you kidding me! Was this a replay from an earlier time? "I can't play with you Deb, people will talk." I just didn't get it.

Again, I turned to food. Do you see a pattern here? We all need to be comforted and loved, and if we can't get it through the healthy route, we become addicted. Sex, gambling, food, or drugs, it doesn't matter; we will become addicts. For me, it was all about the food, and gaining more weight only complicated things. I didn't know how to stop, and by then I didn't want to. After all, food couldn't hurt me, and it wouldn't get angry or pass judgment. In a way, it was the perfect love affair, and who doesn't want that for themselves?

People tend to treat you differently when you're overweight. It's not always about the color of your skin or where you came from. There are lots of different kinds of prejudices. Maybe that's why I understood and had such compassion for those who didn't fit in, according to society's rules.

As the years went on, my life was anything but perfect. My marriage was constantly on rocky ground, while I tried my best to shield my daughter from the insanity. Bill and I broke up and got back together more times than I'd like to admit.

I think I learned early not to judge people. I admired women (and men) who could leave unhappy situations when they weren't working. I could also understand why they stayed. It's never just black and white. I've known many couples on both sides of that coin. *When you judge others, you're also judging yourself, so stop it.*

Nine years after Kelly was born, I gave birth to my son, Jeff. With his big blue eyes and curly blond hair, he was the perfect example of a bouncing baby boy. Because I was overweight, it was hard for people to believe I was pregnant. I was probably the healthiest I had ever been, and I felt great. I joined the YMCA, walked the track daily, and exercised. I craved salads for breakfast, lunch, and dinner. Jeff was nine pounds when he was born, yet I only gained one pound through the entire pregnancy.

I would sing to him on our daily trips to the babysitter. "Sunshine on My Shoulders," by John Denver was his favorite. He'd giggle and try to repeat the words. (Of course, when I mention that today, he's in total denial.) By that time, my husband had lightened up on his drinking, but his temper was still there. Through the drama and the drinking and the verbal abuse, I became more and more withdrawn, while trying my best to raise my children as normally as I could. In some ways, it was the best of times and the worst of times.

How do I know it was meant to happen that way? Because it did.

—Byron Katie

Chapter 7

She Walked in Beauty

Strong and beautiful, with a touch of mischief, is how I would describe Didi. She never took drugs and barely drank, but in one night of undeniable passion, her fate was sealed. My sister, I felt, was another innocent victim in the face of AIDS.

A truly happy person, inside and out, she never spoke an unkind word to or about anyone, and she had many friends. What I admired most about her was how she marched to the beat of her own drummer.

She respected others for who they were but lived her life her own way, regardless of what others thought.

I remember a time when Didi was about fifteen. She was listening to some music in her bedroom, playing the same song, over and over. Mom finally went into her room and said, "If you play 'Jeremiah Was a Bullfrog' one more time, I'm going to take that record and break it!"

Denise was kind of a rebel, so she decided to continue listening to the song…loudly. True to her word, Mom came in and busted the record.

My sister invited a few friends over that night for a small get-together for Jeremiah's passing. Her friends even spoke about what the record meant to them. That was my sister.

Being involved in sports and social activities kept her active, and when she got sick, her life changed drastically. Her vibrancy was gone, and we watched her light dim with each passing day.

I remember visiting her in the hospital on the day she was told she had AIDS. The year was 1987, and this was a "new" disease that most people hadn't heard about. The epidemic was just beginning to take its' toll on the world, and there was mass hysteria everywhere. The thought was that if you went near a person with AIDS, it meant instant death. Rock Hudson, a well-known actor, died from the same disease at the same time my sister was diagnosed. AIDS was originally thought to be a gay man's disease, and they were being beaten unmercifully, especially in New York City. My heart went out to them, but, most of all, my heart ached for my sister.

Denise was treated terribly in the hospital. Nurses were afraid to enter the quarantined room, so they slid the trays of food on the floor, spilling everything. *It seemed obvious to me they were hoping they wouldn't be assigned to take care of her.*

We wore masks and gowns when we visited, and everything was kept quiet. After all, if anyone found out, my family would probably be cast out from society.

It was a scary time for certain. Didi did get better for a while and was able to come home. She lived in the city with her young son, and my family and I took turns visiting as much as we could.

Eventually, she got too sick to take care of herself and had to be moved to a special institution in Philadelphia.

Didi was only twenty-nine years old when she died.

Every time I hear "The Greatest Love" by Whitney Houston, I think of her. The words remind me so much of her. She surely "lived as she believed."

Going through this experience seemed to have drained the life out of everyone that knew and loved her. For years, I read the papers and watched the news, hoping to hear that a cure had been found.

One morning when I went into work, someone, thinking they were being funny and not knowing anything about my sister, left a big note on my desk. It read, "Due to the recent outbreak of AIDS, there will be no ass-kissing in this office." Wow! I couldn't even begin to describe the gut-wrenching disgust I felt. But I said nothing. After all, we had to keep it a secret, right? Today, they have drugs and healthy protocols that can keep people with AIDS alive for years. It was too late for my sister.

When you ask if a heart can be broken, I say it can, but it can also be healed. Time heals, and love and compassion heal, but it takes time. Your strength is inside of you. We all need something to believe in, even when it seems like we can't go on another day. Find your strength in love (thanks, Whitney). Find your belief in what you trust, whether it is God or Buddha or the universe. My beliefs were the only thing that could get me through, and it didn't happen overnight. It took years.

There's an old book called **The Dark Night of the Soul** written by St. John of the Cross, a mystic from the sixteenth century.

Essentially, he says that we go through these dark times, triggered by a sense of hopelessness or nothing going right in our lives, such as the death of a loved one. It can show up as depression and take us to a deep place in our souls. What's happening though is a rebirth, a transformation of self, and eventually, we emerge stronger than we were. What's important to know is that we go through these changes more than once. I look at this as a time of reflection and contemplation.

When I'm hurt or feel really down about something—and I'm talking big hurt here, not little hurt—I step back, take a breath, and say, "Uh oh. I know what's going on here; it's another dark night." Just acknowledging the fact allows me to know it will eventually get better. The God force, your higher self (or whatever your personal belief) is reacting to your pain. In other words, there is a deep healing going on inside of you, right down to your soul, and you don't even know it. You must trust that it's working. For me, this is where meditation comes in, and that could mean different things to you. I think about things like the beauty in my life, what I am or could be grateful for, and how lucky I am to be here on this journey as I learn lessons, and experience all that I am meant to. When I look at it in this way, I literally explode with more love and joy that could only come from cleansing the soul. Does that make sense to you?

Meditation for Deep Healing

Just sit back in your chair, or wherever you're comfortable, and relax. I suggest you don't lie down. You just may nod off; that's o.k. too. Trust the process. Ideally, you could either record it or have someone read it to you, slowly, pausing often.

I'd like you to gently breathe in and breathe out, and if your mind wanders, just bring it back to the breath.

Through your breath, I'd like you to bring your awareness into your belly. Breathe in a beautiful healing light, and breathe out any stress or negativity that you may be holding. As you continue breathing in and out, following the natural rhythm of your body, imagine a large white bubble in front of you. The bubble is misty and looks as though a gentle fog is moving around inside, like the early morning dew on a lake. Notice this mist swirling around and around as you slowly walk towards the bubble.

As you continue your gentle breathing in and out, you instinctively know that you're safe, and you walk into the bubble, breathing in a beautiful and protective white light. This light surrounds your entire body and you know you are in a place of complete love. There is nothing else that exists here. Feel the love that surrounds you as you release all tension, all worries. Breathe in the healing energy, and feel it cleansing every organ, and every cell in your body. You feel an inner peace like you've never felt before. Stay with this feeling for a few minutes, continuously focusing on the breath.

If you choose, you may bring other people into your bubble, but only if you want to. Is there someone you're thinking of, someone who you'd like to share these feelings of love and joy with? See them now, in your mind's eye and allow them to enter your sacred space. Do they need healing too? Just notice them. If you choose, you may share a glance or a gentle smile. Allow them to breathe in the healing light from your bubble and welcome them. That person is also a part of you.

Thank your friends for being there, and, when you're ready, allow them to move on.

Once again, you're here on your own, inside the bubble. Enjoy your time here. A deep healing is taking place. Take as much time as you need, and, when you're ready, take a few deep breaths, in and out.

A gentle breeze on your face gently blows the bubble behind and away from you. There's nothing you need to do but breathe, as the pure white light disappears into the energy of the universe. When you're ready, gently open your eyes, and thank your guides for this experience.

Life begins at the end of your comfort zone.

—Neale Donald Walsh

Chapter 8

How Do I Fix This?

My bad eating habits, my only source of internal comfort, continued, and my weight ballooned to over two hundred pounds. I never saw it coming. Sound familiar?

I didn't know what to do; how to fix my eating issues. I did the gym thing, over and over. I tried every diet I could think of. I went to doctors and tried the diet-pill route again. I listened to friends and family and tried, out of desperation, some unconventional methods. Everything worked for a short while, and then I was back to where I started. Classic yo-yo syndrome.

Once, my husband, in one of his short outbursts, reiterated to me how lucky I was to have found him, because no one else would want me. Did I even have to question why I still carried those lingering self-esteem issues around? I don't think there's anyone who doesn't have excess baggage to carry; do you?

It's funny though, from childhood right up to being an adult, I never placed blame on anyone but me. Today, I see things differently and realize there's no blame here, just different people trying to live their lives in the only ways they can or know how to. That doesn't mean people don't have to take responsibility for their actions; they do. I, or you, just don't have to buy into someone else's drama.

One day, after being married for over twenty years, an overwhelming case of positivity came over me. I don't know, maybe it was all the prayer; maybe it was all the comfort food. I woke up with this thought that life isn't meant to be lived this way. "*It's not supposed to be like this,*" I said to myself.

Over the years, we did try counseling, AA meetings, and anything else I could think of that might help. They all seemed to be temporary fixes. I knew something was changing. Something different was happening, and, although the unknown frightened me, I looked forward to the movement, in whatever way it came.

It took another two years, but I finally found the courage to say, "I'm done. I'm out of here!" My kids needed their sanity, and we all deserved to be happy.

My life didn't change drastically, and it didn't get easier, but I was free. For the first time, I felt like I could take a deep breath in, and, when I let it out, I was OK. What I can tell you though, with certainty, is that there were a lot of forks in the road. I stumbled, I fell, I bruised, but I never looked back. Besides, it was time to call on my resources. All that I had learned over the years could now begin to serve me. At least, that's what I hoped.

The court awarded custody of my son to his dad, and I still wasn't emotionally strong enough to fight him. He had money. Period.

Jeff finally came to live with me when he was eighteen, which made me happy. He left right away to go to school in North Carolina, but, when he came home, it was to me.

Little by little, I began changing, and my life took a different course. I questioned everything. Having a newfound desire to learn as much as I could and not having an interest in the mundane college experience, I started to explore metaphysical studies. "Why am I here, and what is my purpose?" Although strange and new to most people, I was fascinated by natural healing. I studied things with funny names like fêng shui* (fung-shway) and Reiki* (ray-kee).

I studied meditation, hypnosis, and spirituality. I learned how to step out of my comfort zone with motivational guru Tony Robbins, even working for him for a few years. Twenty years ago, it wasn't fashionable to know this stuff, and today it's more mainstream.

I spent lots of money studying and got a ridiculous number of certifications. I became the proverbial student, a moniker that followed me for years, much to my dismay.

Feng-Shui – The study of how our surroundings influence our daily lives. Clear Your Clutter with Feng-Shui – Karen Kingston.

Reiki - A subtle yet powerful 3000 year-old energy system based on gentle touch, also known as Therapeutic Touch; used to balance the bodys' natural ability to heal.

It seemed like I couldn't contain my excitement, and I wanted to share all this knowledge with everyone I met, but I couldn't seem to attract the right people. I had a few private clients and did a lot of free workshops, but my marketing skills weren't there. Many of my teachers and fellow students seemed to be successful, writing books, being on TV and radio, and accomplishing so much. I just didn't get it. "Trust yourself, Debbie; you don't give yourself enough credit." Easy words that were tough to follow.

Deciding that I would apply what I learned on myself, I tackled my issues with food. I meditated, made my own hypnosis tapes, and used some of the energy work I had studied. I feng-shuied my life and "tapped*" my way to feeling good. Sure, everything worked for a while, but it never lasted.

Another lesson was brewing in the distance.

Tapping - Technique that stimulates the meridian points by tapping on them with fingertips. The Tapping Solution for Weight Loss and Body Confidence – Jessica Ortner

Nothing ever goes away until it has taught us
what we need to know.

—Pema Chodron
American, Tibetan Buddhist

Chapter 9

Hello, Ego; It's Me Again

Why isn't any of this working for me? I thought. I studied hard
and tried my best and I was still having a difficult time. It didn't
make sense. As I usually do when I'm trying to figure
something out, I went back to basics. My first thought was to
pick up my *Course in Miracles** guide. After all, I'd spent
almost four years studying, but maybe there was something I
missed, or maybe I wasn't ready to hear how that book could
help me at the time.

I began to understand *the difference between knowing and caring.* I knew a lot and shared it, but what I didn't see at first was that my ego got in the way. I know we're all familiar with that side of us. It's the suspicious side, the part that always wants to be in control. It's that part of ourselves that we give our power to. I'll admit, it felt good to share my knowledge with others, but I wondered if it wasn't about "look what I know; see what I can do." The funny thing about working from the ego is that you can never win. After a while, especially when you're working on yourself, you get knocked down a peg from a spiritual perspective. Oh hell, sometimes you get knocked right off the top rung of the ladder! That's your wake-up call. It was for me. I realized that nobody cares what you know, only that you care. It was a tough time for me, and very humbling.

A Course in Miracles – A book written by Helen Shucman, with portions transcribed and edited by William Thetford, containing a curriculum to bring about what it calls a Spiritual Transformation.

Today, I ask for humility in all that I do, and I try my best to come from a place, not of knowing, but of caring. It's helped me to be more authentic and to be able to listen more to others, instead of letting my ego be in control. Oh, I admit, it's still there and will probably always be, but now it takes the back seat when I drive.

Reflections on the Lake

The beach is always so serene and peaceful in the evenings. Summer hasn't quite started yet. Soft billowy clouds seem to pierce the evening sky, and the sun begins to fade. Looking down through the sandy marsh, I see two fishermen casting their lines out onto the glimmering lake. What a perfect scene. A child's voice on the other side of the lake squeals with happiness as she splashes about and pays little care to the fact that the water is still cold.

As I look out over the lake, sitting in my old, comfortable red beach chair, I get a sense that everything is all right with the world, at least for the moment.

Sometimes it feels like this island earth is just a big puzzle, and it's up to us to figure out where the pieces go.

Here, deep in my thoughts, it's like an island too; a place of wonder and interlocking pieces. How many people are out there, feeling that they don't fit into this very complex system we call life. Sometimes I wonder how much beauty is stored inside of us, never to be opened, because of the fear of being judged or feeling not good enough.

Society, in general, is tough on those who don't fit in. You'll always know if you are, or have ever been, one of them. I know I've been there, many times. There's that little boy at the bus stop who stands alone while groups of friends gather at the other end. There's the teenager wondering why everyone's going to the prom but her, and the child who gets bullied because he's "different." And then there are the grown-ups who never seem to get it together.

You see, it never was about the food.

When I was in school studying to be a health coach, I had an amazing teacher. Joshua* always said, "Why try to fit in, when it's so much easier and better to just fit out?" Think about it. For me, these were words to live by.

Who decided we were different? Who gets to decide, and who do you turn to when you feel like your heart hurts, and you just can't get the words out?

Sometimes I can't get the words out. Right now, I'm just thinking out loud.

Instead of going home right after work today, I decided to go to one of the area lakes. We have quite a few here in southern Jersey where I live. I haven't had much time to relax, so I'm making it a priority for the next hour or two. I may do some reading, writing, or even meditating. Have you ever meditated? It helps me when I've had a stressful day. Getting clear on my thoughts is another bonus.

This lake is beautiful, and so big. A gentle breeze wraps around me as I close my eyes for a moment and just breathe.

There's a lone baby duck swimming not far from where I am.

The last time I was here, it was cold and rainy, and there was

a parade of mom, dad, and eleven baby ducks gliding on the

water. It was the perfect formation.

A foghorn sounds from across the lake, but I can't see

anyone. Right here, right now, all is perfect.

As I drift into the next chapter of my life (some would call it the

golden years), I realize that this life, my life, has taught me so

much. I look at things differently now. There's such a calm, an

inner peace, and, with that, comes a sense of entitlement that

a younger generation doesn't get to know right away.

Joshua Rosenthal – Founder of IIN (Institute for Integrative Nutrition), the worlds' largest Nutrition school and certification program for Health and Wellness Coaching

I see so much joy in practicing love and acceptance, in spite of what I believed my imperfections were. As I get older, I learn to embrace the real me, authentic and unique in my own way. I don't seem to be as hard on myself as I used to be. Learning to accept and love others exactly as they are has helped to open up a whole new world of possibilities.

There's a small group of youngsters across the lake. A young man is singing and playing guitar for them. It sounds like some good old-fashioned folk music, the kind I used to listen to when I was younger. *How could I have not noticed all the beauty in the world?*

I feel so grown up lately. What does that even mean? Well, my choices are my own, and, although I listen and respect others opinions, ultimately, I make my own decisions; that's a good feeling. Do you agree? I've also given up the need to control others, and I just let them be. Since practicing things like love and forgiveness, I've come into my own.

Removing myself from negativity and toxic relationships took a while, but, when that happened, I began to heal. The experience of self-love allowed me to be the person I am today, someone I'm much happier with. Does that mean everything's perfect? Not at all. It means I'm evolving, in my own way and in my own time.

I have so much to be grateful for. It could be anything…something as simple as the sun shining through my window (or winning with some scratch-offs).

It's all about finding ways to be happy and having some fun along the way. Dare to be different, don't take life too seriously, and know that loving yourself is always the best kind of love. *I hope you travel lightly; don't take life too seriously; and just be the authentic, unique, and beautiful person you were born to be.*

Strive for continuous improvement instead of perfection.

—Kim Collins
track and field sprinter

Chapter 10

Kushi and I

Once upon a time, when I was in my late thirties, I stumbled upon some information about whole-foods cooking and what they termed a *macrobiotic* community.* I thought *hmm, maybe there's something to this whole-food thing, or maybe I'm just going to blow more money on something that's not working. Yeah, Deb, there's that power of positive thinking again!*

I signed up for a one-week Way to Health* course and was off to the Kushi Institute* in Becket, Massachusetts. I was, and still am, terrible with directions, and, back then, there were no cell phones or GPSes. What should have been a five-hour ride was almost doubled, and, by the time I arrived, I had a splitting headache. It never dawned on me that it might have been all the Dunkin' Donuts and coffee I downed, trying to stay awake. So much for healthy eating.

The Berkshire Mountains were beautiful, and, once my headache settled down, I relaxed and appreciated the peacefulness and calm that this place exuded.

*Kushi Institute – Leading Macrobiotic educational center in Becket, Massachusetts, founded by Michio and Aveline Kushi.

*Macrobiotics – A whole foods, mostly plant based way of eating, considering a persons' health, climate, age, gender, geography.

*Way to Health - Program at Kushi Institute for people who would like to use macrobiotics to support recovery from serious illness or for a quick start to optimize good health.

What a delicious and diverse group of people. Some were there to heal from major illness and others to learn a healthier lifestyle. Except for being overweight, I was in amazingly good health. When I got home, I felt like a new person. The cooking classes I took while there helped to keep me on track, and I maintained that lifestyle for a while. I cooked everything fresh, ate only organic and made sure I ate according to the seasons. I lost some weight, but more importantly, I felt so good. I looked younger, my skin was clear and soft, and my energy was amazing.

After about six months of being a "crazy vegan macro," I realized it was unrealistic for me to live this type of lifestyle twenty-four/seven. I was working two jobs, and, by the time I got all the prep and cooking done, it was eleven or twelve at night. I was too tired to eat, and let's not forget how expensive organic food was.

I was always the type of person who had to do something perfectly or not at all. My thoughts were so foolish. *Why do we put so much pressure on ourselves to be perfect?*

Today I know better. We never need to get it right, we just have to try, and we have to care about what we put into our bodies. There are ways around things, meaning, yes, some foods should absolutely be organic and local, and others can be conventional. If you're interested, you can go online and look up the Environmental Worker's Group* (EWG). They are updating information all the time, so it's good to download the app* to your phone. You'll get lots of great info and most importantly a list called "The Dirty Dozen". Those are foods you should avoid unless they're organic. I still believe the old adage, "Knowledge is power," so get some info, and then trust yourself to make the choices that are right for you.

*Environmental Worker's Group (EWG) - A group dedicated to make people aware of the chemicals we're being exposed to, everything from food to shampoos. ** The EWG Living App makes it easy. You can scan a product, review it's rating and pick a better choice.

I'd like to share something here that I've learned. The stress of trying to be perfect and trying to do the right thing is exhausting. I always wanted to "get it right," but there's no such thing. Over time, I realized that stressing out over something does more harm to your body than anything you can feed it. I stand by that belief, because it's all I can do, and I know it's enough. There are so many other areas of your life, and they all need to work in harmony. How are your relationships, your finances, your spiritual or religious beliefs? Do you get enough exercise, or any at all? All these things matter to bring you balance. And you know what? You're gonna screw up! Remember that we're here to learn, not get it perfect. I carry a small card in my pocket that I had laminated. It reads, "I don't need to be perfect, I just need to be better than I was the day before." Just recently I've added a more spiritual quote that I absolutely love: "God, please put the next step in front of me that's aligned for my path in a way I can understand", and then I let go. Maybe you have a quote or loving thought that you could carry in your wallet too.

I don't need to be perfect...

I just need to be better than I was

The day before.

Wayne Dyer

So here I am, feeling like a failure, again. Still overweight, still unhappy, and still emotionally spent. What now? As the years went by, I tried to adhere to a healthy lifestyle. My weight went up and down but mostly stayed the same. I shifted back and forth from vegan to vegetarianism to adding meat and dairy and back again. My eating was so erratic, and it was all I could focus on. I was miserable. I hated being fat. I hated being lonely.

My daughter was away at school. My son lived with his dad. My finances were less than desirable. I hated my job. Anything else? I could make a list. God, I was always making lists. Why couldn't I just be happy? Why couldn't I meet someone nice, someone who could be a part of my team, loving each other, supporting each other, and then together helping others to make lasting change in their lives? Why? Why not? How would you answer my why? Note to self: There's that damn ego again, Debbie. *Get over yourself.*

The most beautiful people we have known are those who have known defeat, suffering, struggle and loss, and have found their way out of the depths. Beautiful people do not just happen.

—Elisabeth Kübler-Ross

Chapter 11

The Diagnosis

Fast forward to 2013. By now I had been working at a large retail store for about fifteen years. I wasn't happy there, and knowing this place was toxic took its toll on me.

On one particular day, I was working with a customer, when I got a call on my cell phone. I had a breast biopsy a few days earlier and was waiting for a call from my doctor.

"Hi, Deb. It's Dr. Farro," he said. "You've got breast cancer. We'll get you set up for surgery right away, and then the radiation. Good news, though. I don't think you'll need chemo."

What? What just happened? What did I just hear? How could this doctor speak so matter-of-factly about something so serious? I was numb.

"Please excuse me," I said to my customer. "I'll get someone to finish up." I ran to the back of the building as quickly as my tears were falling. An overwhelming fear of the unknown swept through my body like a cold winter storm.

Within a few minutes, I regained my composure and breathed normally. "OK, Debbie. Just breathe. Breathe and relax." Right then, a thought came to me. *Where do I go when I want to heal in a natural and loving way? I'm going back to Becket, to the Kushi Institute. They've helped so many people heal from serious illnesses; surely they can help me.*

OK, Universe, Do Your Thing!

Although two things were not in my favor, time off and money, I knew I was going, and that's where I would start. I took a break, went to my car, and called the Kushi Institute. A week-long class was starting the following weekend. *It's Monday, I* thought. *There's still some time to pull this together.*

The company I worked for required three-weeks' notice for a day off, unless, of course, it was an emergency. It was definitely that! My next dilemma was the price. I needed to come up with at least one thousand dollars, of which I had none.

When I arrived home and checked my messages, there was one from a friend I hadn't seen in a while. The message was, "Deb, give me a call. I need to know your address." *O.k., I* thought. *Maybe there's a wedding coming up.* Sara wasn't home when I called back, so I left the information on her voicemail.

Three days later, I received a check for one thousand dollars! There was a note attached that read, "Thank you so much for lending me this money. I know it's been a while, and I'm able to send it now." Wow…synchronicity at its best.

I was going to Kushi!

The next step was to call my daughter and let her know what was going on. Kelly was always supportive of me, so she wasn't surprised by my decision. I'm sure she was worried, but she never let on.

The next day I was on my way.

Naturally I was frightened. A cancer diagnosis is nothing to take lightly. The difference was that I had done so much spiritual work on myself by then that my beliefs were stronger than my fear. I wanted to heal, and I wanted to do it without bombarding my body with poisons if I could help it.

Hoping to gain some clarity, I began the strict macrobiotic lifestyle that I had started so long ago. Who knew I'd be back almost twenty years later with a need to relook at my life.

I knew, with an unwavering certainty that this is where I needed to be, at least for a while. I studied, ate, cooked, meditated, and immersed myself in the beauty of the mountains. My life was different now. I knew I would never be the same again, and that was fine with me. Soul-searching became my newfound friend.

On about the second day there, I stumbled upon a book called *Dying to Be Me* by Anita Moorjani. It was about a young woman riddled with cancer and a grim diagnosis. While she was in the hospital, she claims she visited heaven and has quite a story to tell. Her message is one of hope: "Just live your life." Today, completely cancer free, she travels the world, telling her beautiful and inspiring story.

While at Kushi, I made the decision to have surgery as soon as I got home; a decision I gave a lot of thought to. The nurses were in shock when I came out of anesthesia easily. "I'm hungry," was the first thing I said. Pushing away the sugar-laden Jell-O, chicken salad, and ginger ale,

I opted for the meal my daughter brought me. It consisted of miso soup, brown rice, and greens. My body had been clean, and I was feeling great. I wasn't about to screw it up.

I can't say I was ever sick, because I always felt good. I knew the next decision would be hard. The doctor said I had to have radiation. Once again, I read, I researched, and I prayed. I was terrified when I made the decision not to have it, but I knew in my gut that it was the right decision for me. My weight loss was steady, and friends began asking me if I was all right. They were concerned the cancer was still there, and I had a hard time convincing them otherwise. *Silly me*, I thought. *Why am I trying to convince anyone about anything? It's all about me anyway, right?*

By the time all was said and done, I had lost almost seventy pounds and felt wonderful. I started getting compliments on how good I looked, and people asked what I did to take care of myself. I was happy to share what I had learned with anyone who asked.

Kelly, my daughter, was such a great cook. By then, she knew as much as I did about whole foods. Her "feel-good" soups were amazing, and she made them for me every day.

By the time I got back to work, I was happy and thankful, and I looked at having cancer as a blessing. My body was protecting me, telling me it was time to wake up and do something. Remember, I was stubborn, but my future checkups proved I had made the right decision.

My daughter and I started a small whole-foods cooking class in my home. Although we got rave reviews, it never quite took off. Unfortunately, neither one of us had the time we needed to devote to the business. We both worked full-time jobs and had to travel each week to get fresh local, organic food. Maybe my marketing was off, or maybe it just wasn't the right time. No worries though; it was all just a part of the plan. You know, I just had a thought. Maybe I should've taken a class in marketing too! Interesting.

Kelly's What's Left in the Fridge Soup

Ingredients

8 cups water

8 teaspoons white miso

5 carrots, peeled and roughly

chopped

3 stalks celery, chopped

1 to 2 clove garlic, minced

1 medium onion, chopped

1 cup chopped broccoli

1 cup diced butternut squash

1 tablespoon olive or coconut oil

pinch of salt

Directions

Sauté onion in olive oil with salt.

Add garlic; sauté 4 minutes.

Add carrots; sauté 4 minutes.

Add celery; sauté 4 minutes.

Add butternut squash; sauté 5 minutes.

Add broccoli and water.

Bring to boil; lower to simmer.

Simmer on low flame 15 minutes or until carrots are tender.

Remove ¼ cup of water to dissolve white miso paste.

Put miso in bowl, add water, use fork to dissolve miso, and add
back to pot.

*(Be sure to only simmer on low for 5 minutes, and do not let water
come to a boil once the miso is added)*

If needed, add more miso to taste. It should not be overly salty,
but should be flavorful.

Enjoy!

*Visit **kellyryanskitchen** on Instagram for some awesome
healthy food ideas.

A Tickle from Heaven

Hello, my loved ones. Did you know that you're perfect just as you are, and you were never created to be anything less? You are loved beyond measure. You do know that, don't you? My creation, my beauty, you are here to illuminate the world. I've given you the most amazing gifts from my heart, so do not think that your love could be any less than mine.

I know you've strayed, and your choices were not understood, but you'll find your way in time. It must be so. I am all things. I am your light.

That mark on your face, on your body, the one you call an imperfection, is a tickle from me, a tickle from heaven, so smile and wear it proudly. Right now, today, know that you are exactly as you should be. I see you, and I see love. I see you, a reflection of me. For each step you take and each hill you climb, celebrate. Celebrate who you are. When you reach the top of that mountain, and you will, stand tall and stand proud for all to see, and then look around and know that you have found your place in the world and know we are all here with you, and you are and will always be, my child.

With love, and heaven sent...Me.

The above message was taken from one of my many journals of channeling and writings from the heart. This one was especially dear to me.

You can journal this with dreams too. Keep a pad and pen on your nightstand. When you awake, write down what you remember. Neatness does not count, and it doesn't have to make sense. We forget our dreams quickly, so do this right away. In a months' time, go back and reread what you wrote. See if you can find a pattern. Your dreams are always trying to tell you something.

One of my favorite dream books is 'Inner Work' by Robert Johnson; Using Dreams and Active Imagination for Personal Growth.

The hardest moments are the call to something greater.

—author unknown

Chapter 12

Sometimes Life Sucks

For a while, it seemed like everything was going well, beginning to fall into place. Then all the craziness started. There were medical bills and credit cards and stress, stress, stress. My paycheck, although not terrible, just wasn't cutting it. It became more and more difficult to purchase good, healthy food—at least the kind I chose to eat. I bought what I could afford and began making poor food choices, gaining back a lot of the weight I had lost. That put me in a terrible depression.

Payments were late, and I eventually lost my home and moved into a rental in another town.

I woke up one day in terrible pain and went to the emergency room. It was sciatica. Anyone who's ever had that can understand how painful it is. A few weeks into therapy, I was back in the emergency room with a different kind of pain. This time it was shingles. I had to stop therapy until it went away, which was a long time. I can't sugarcoat this. It hurt like hell! *Sometimes life sucks!* Stress can do that to you.

Finally, after a week or so I had to get back to work, pain and all. It reinforced the fact that I didn't want to be there. To me, everyone, customers and associates, were always angry, and you could feel the negativity floating around the building like a heavy fog that never lifted. Like any other place, there were a few that were just mean, but, for the most part they were good people. There was one special person I had met when I first started with the company.

The best teachers are those who show you where to look but don't tell you what to see.

—Alexandra K. Trenfor
Web quotes

Chapter 13

A Friend for All Seasons

"The wind beneath my wings", to quote Bette Midler.

Karen and I were destined to meet, and our friendship would become what I consider one of the greatest lessons in my life. Fifteen years earlier, I had just started working at a large retail store. I was in a new town, and didn't know anyone. After being married for over twenty years, my husband and I were winding down to living our lives separately. It was a bittersweet time of both sadness from the past and excitement for new beginnings.

Karen and I both started working together in April 1998. *It was funny how we sort of bumped into each other.* I needed to use the restroom and as I pushed open the door, I heard this deep grumbling sound of someone yelling. "I hate this place," she said. "I can't even get a day off. My sister lives in Pennsylvania, and God forbid I get to spend some time with her."

As I looked around, I noticed there was no one else there. My demeanor was a little different. I was more on the quiet and shy side, even a little withdrawn. I'm sure that came from all my self-esteem issues growing up.

As I saw this petite woman with long, chestnut-brown hair leaning over the sink and throwing water on her face, I decided to say something. "Why don't you go to visit your sister, if that's what you want to do?" I said. "You deserve to do something that makes you happy, don't you?"

She looked up, turned to me with her piercing green eyes and said, "You're right. Why don't I?"

And that's how we met.

Fast forward to April 2014. I was at work when I got the call.

"Hi, Debbie, it's Gina, Karen's daughter. I just wanted to call and tell you Mom died last night."

It had been almost a year since I had seen Karen, and I never knew she was battling breast cancer. Our friendship was like that. Sometimes we got together almost every day and sometimes not for months. This time it was longer than usual. For a moment, it felt like my heart stopped beating. I never knew. I had called numerous times and left messages. I just assumed she was busy. The guilt of not being there was unbearable. She never knew I was battling the same illness. I should have told her. I should have tried.

Karen was a perfectionist, and the type of person who could do anything. She was a builder and a cook and an artist, to name a few. I remember waiting in a hotel room when her daughter got married. True to form, Karen sat down at the piano and started playing it. I had known her over ten years at that time and never knew she could play the piano.

Being a private person, she kept a lot to herself. I knew her husband had died years earlier in a tragic car accident and that she went on to raise the two girls alone.

Our friendship was unique in that we were complete opposites. I remember her younger daughter saying to me, "I don't know how you guys are such good friends when you're so different."

That is exactly why we were such good friends. We saw differences in each other that we lacked in ourselves. Karen was funny and crazy most of the time, and her nutty shenanigans always left me laughing hysterically. I, on the other hand, was a quiet, reserved, and sensitive type. We were both extreme in our ways, and I now know why we were brought together...to balance each other out. *Simply put, I needed her craziness, and she needed my quiet.*

Once when we were taking a trip to Hershey, Pennsylvania, I started whistling. Karen, in an alarmed voice said, "What's that you're doing? Are you trying to whistle?"

Yes, I was.

"Look, I don't know who taught you that, but you're gonna learn it the right way, so start practicing!"

That was a *really* long trip, but you know what? Today I can whistle with the best of them! She would be so proud. Over the years' we had so much fun together, and it was always good seeing her.

I didn't know anyone at her funeral except for the immediate family. How could Karen and I have been so close for so long, yet I had never met any of her friends? What a strange friendship we had. It was months before I got to talk to her oldest daughter, and it felt so good to speak with her about her mom. I told Angela how I knew she was still here watching over us. I told her how I walked around Manahawkin Lake each day before work, talking with my best friend. We had walked through that park together, and it was the only way I knew to honor her memory.

My memories of Karen are the ones I carry with me, close to my heart. She was my rock. She was always there when I needed a friend, and helped me through some rough times.

Her dedication and love for her family was amazing. Her compassion for animals was beautiful to watch. I admired her for so many things, and especially how she never judged anyone. She taught me how to just live in the moment, always reminding me to stop and smell the roses. Those who were lucky enough to have met her were lucky enough. She was put here for a purpose, and, for me, she will always be my greatest teacher.

Your need for acceptance can make
you invisible in this world...
risk being seen in all your glory.

—Jim Carrey

Chapter 14

What's Love Really About Anyway?

For the longest time, I ached for love in my life. I certainly had
the love of family, but I wanted the Hallmark kind of love, a
real relationship. I wanted to have deep and meaningful
conversations and to share my life with someone special,
even though I was scared to death of being intimate again. It
had been so long, and my past surely wasn't something that I
could look at with any kind of expertise. What could I possibly
know about dating?

After some hesitation and a lot of encouragement from my friends, I joined an online dating site. OK, more than one. It was interesting, to say the least, but I was determined to put myself out there and see if anything developed.

And so I began dating. I could probably write a complete chapter on "Dating Adventures for the Unaware." I really got a chuckle out of the "FWB" (friends with benefits) guys I spoke with; so glad I figured that one out before the date. Then there were the ones I hoped I didn't meet up with, namely, the scammers. Oh yeah, I did, three times in a row! You'd think I would have figured it out upfront. But I did figure it out, sooner than later. *Darn*, I thought. *They sure wrote some nice love letters*.

I did have a lot of fun and met some very nice guys, but after about a year or so, I had enough. *Alright*, I thought; *time to nip self-doubt in the bud*.

Ugh! That Self-Doubt Thing…*Really*?

What is self-doubt anyway? The best relationship we can have is the one we have with ourselves, and it could never be more than that. *A Course in Miracles* tells us that entering into a relationship is a holy encounter, and when our ego and self-doubt move out of the way, we can let go and relax. It's only us attracting ourselves, isn't it? It all comes down to *self-love*.

"What I see in you is also in me," - *A Course in Miracles.*

Then I Met Joe

What first attracted me to Joe was that he was soft-spoken and reserved. He was retired and helped a lot when Hurricane Sandy hit the Jersey Shore. We met at a meet up for singles. Earlier that night, my vertigo kicked in and I wasn't feeling well, but since I promised a few friends I'd meet them there, I made an effort to "get it together." When I arrived, I was relieved to be feeling better, but decided to forego the wine, just in case.

"Over here, Debbie," my girlfriend yelled from across the room. "We have a table. This is Joe, and he's going to sit with us tonight."

By the time my other friends arrived, he and I were talking and enjoying one another's company. It was the first time in a long time I felt comfortable with someone.

The next day, he came into the store where I worked and asked me out for lunch. We wound up dating for a few months, and it felt good to spend time with him.

Unfortunately, the red flags were already up. I just chose not to see them. What I did see was someone I considered to be a gentleman with an old-school charm. We were alike in so many ways that I was just "pulled into" the story. At some point, I guess I did something you're not supposed to do, at least relative to the good old "dating standards." Yes, I did it, I told him how much I enjoyed his company, and I told him how nice it was to have someone's' arms around me, and how much I liked hugs. I guess I caught him off-guard, but I knew what I wanted and what I deserved.

"Thanks for opening up," he said. "It was really nice, and I'm glad you did." It was simple and honest, and it was over.

After Joe, all my insecurities came back and hit me like a brick. God, I thought I was over that. I thought that this area in my life would finally work; I'd finally be happy. I began to question myself. "What did I say? What did I do? Was it me? Was it him? Did I talk too much, not enough, should I call him? Was he thinking of me?" And I rambled on, allowing my inner child to take charge again.

Time and distance allow us the opportunity to look back at different situations, and for me, it was the model of how I thought things should work or play out; but that wasn't reality.

What I've learned, through a series of different types of relationships and dating (remember those websites?), is that no matter what you're looking for, it's better to be less serious and more playful. It's not about looking for "the one," but enjoying the moment. It doesn't mean you're giving up your dreams or desires, or even putting them on hold. What happens is that you become more lighthearted and see that there's a reason you meet different people in your life. I was always such a serious person, so learning to "lighten up" was something I had issues with, but I was up for the challenge.

I could decide to be angry and unhappy and blame others for my past, but did I want to bring that kind of baggage into a new relationship, or even just a friendship? Hell no! We, you and I, deserve better, so if I were to share anything that I've learned, it would be to have fun and enjoy the process.

One day, when you're relaxing and not thinking too much, but just feeling good and being in the moment, you might meet your perfect match, if you haven't already. When that happens, you'll see how easy and effortless it all becomes, and the experience will feel refreshing, joyful, and right.

Letter to My Inner Child

Hello, dear one,

Are you there? I know it's been a long road and sometimes a tough one too. We've come a long way, you and I. It might have seemed that I wasn't always there for you, and I know you felt so alone and scared. I'm sorry for that, but I'm here now, and you don't have to ever feel like that again. I'll protect you, and I'll keep you safe; I promise. It's OK to let your guard down. The past is what's made you strong, and I'm so proud of you. I know you held on to so much, including the excess weight. I understand it was a way to protect yourself from being hurt, but you don't need to do that anymore.

You're here now, and I'm here, and together, we're all grown up. We can now let go of the past and all that we thought was real. Nothing real could ever be threatened*, and now that you know that, you can come out of hiding and be your beautiful, authentic self. You don't have to be afraid of who you are anymore or what others think of you. It's none of our business what they think anyway.

You don't need to be fixed. Never did. I'll hold your hand when you need me to, and together we'll be stronger and happier and sillier and all the things we want to be. I promise you it will be more than OK.

Thank you for being you and for helping me become the person I am today. I am honored and blessed that you have been a part of my life.

I love you. Your Grown-Up Self

*Taken from A Course in Miracles

Experiencing different relationships got me to thinking a lot about choices and how we have no control over another person, let alone the power to decide how they're going to feel about someone or something.

I could choose to be upset, or I could choose to love, regardless of whether it worked out with that person or not. I chose love. I chose to open my heart and let the energy, like a winding river, find its own path. What became most important was that I was learning to love myself. *Like a thief in the night, another lesson had come and gone.*

Today, I recognize how important it is to take it easy on ourselves. Keep loving; keep trying. I know sometimes it sounds like a foo-foo phrase, and I felt the same way until I got out of my own way.

It's amazing how your heart opens a little more each day.

There will always be days when you feel like saying, "What's the use? I'm tired, tired of trying." There will be days when you feel like you're slipping back into your old habits.

There will also be days of feeling great and funny and of being silly just because you can. I love those days and take full advantage of them. I sing out loud and dance in the rain and do things that make me feel good.

What makes you feel good? Is it the sunshine on your face or the sand in your toes? Is it the sound of your children laughing? Is it watching an old movie and eating popcorn, or calling an old friend and reminiscing? What about bear hugs and kisses and spending the day with someone you love? For me, it's all those things and more.

Meditation:

The Secret Place

Sit back, relax, and take a breath in and out. Just breathe gently in and out, and, as you close your eyes, let your breath relax you, your head, your neck. Relax your shoulders and your arms. Relax your stomach, your legs, your feet. Breathe in and out, and relax your entire body.

Imagine yourself walking through a path in the woods as you feel the warmth of the suns' rays on your skin. Slowly breathe in those rays, deeply into your belly, and breathe out any negativity or tension you may still be holding.

After a few minutes of walking, you see a tree. You notice it has an opening, and, as you get closer, you see a beautiful staircase carved into the tree. You begin to descend down the stairs, down, down, around and around the spiral staircase you go. A few more steps, and you reach the bottom. There's a door in front of you. You open it. What do you see?

Notice it now. This is your place. Your private oasis. A place of your very own that you can return to again and again if you choose to. You may create this place anyway you like. Are there benches and books or gardens filled with flowers? Are there animals around? Is there a lake or mountains or both?

Look around. Maybe you like the ocean and the warm sand on your feet. Take a few minutes now to create your special place.

This is where you can go to relax and rest, just to get away. Spend as much time there as you like.

Now it's time to come back. Say good-bye to your secret place, and head back toward the tree. Climb back up the steps until you reach the top. *As you walk back down the path, you once again feel the warmth of the sun on your face. You know you can go back to your special place anytime you like just by closing your eyes and thinking about it.* Take a few deep breaths in and out, and, when you're ready, open your eyes.

Little by little I started, feeling better once again. If there was one thing I had, it was perseverance. I may have tired out, but I never gave up and never stopped trying. Somewhere deep inside of me, I knew that if I changed the way I reacted to situations, they would improve, and I could start feeling better about myself and that maybe I could finally get a handle on this eating issue.

And I said to my body softly, "I want to be your friend." It took a long breath and replied, "I have been waiting my whole life for this."

—Maya Angelou

Chapter 15

Everything's Better When You're Dancing

I'd always wanted to dance. Oh sure, I moved around on the dance floor, but I never really knew how to dance. I searched the Internet and found the perfect place to learn, and it was only ten minutes from my house. Better yet, I didn't need a partner, a requirement with some dance studios. So I began to learn ballroom dance.

I was both nervous and excited. After all, the last time I had danced with a man, I was nineteen, and he accused me of stepping all over his feet. As you can imagine, I was embarrassed as hell. *Wasn't gonna do that again*, I thought, but this time I was determined.

You know what? I loved it, and I was so sorry I hadn't taken dance lessons years ago. The nicest thing was that I got to dance with every man there! I was ecstatic and had so much fun. I laughed...it felt so good to laugh.

Twice a year, the studio puts on a showcase for the community, and I decided to join them. I learned a dance routine that included a group of women, a ladies' formation. We practiced every week for six months to get the routine down. It was a go-go routine from the sixties and the costumes were a real stretch for me (pun intended). You can see a picture on my Instagram page (debwithgrace) The morning of the performance was exciting and nerve-wracking, but we got through it (I think the wine helped a bit), and we had a blast.

Learning to dance gave me the confidence to go out and meet people. When I get asked out on the dance floor now, I say yes, instead of the usual, "No thanks." It's such a liberating feeling to move your body in a beautiful and sexy way, and I can't wait to learn the tango!

What's your favorite dance?

Not all those who
wander are lost.

—J. R. R. Tolkien
English Writer, Poet

Chapter 16

Starting Over Again

After about seventeen years of working at a large retail firm, I was let go. All I could say was, "Thank you." I had known for some time that I was leaving that environment. Nothing is ever in vain, and my job there was done. A new kind of peace washed over me as I walked to my car that day. Another journey had begun. It was the journey to happiness. The journey to a place called home.

Leaving work gave me a new sense of freedom. I had time to reflect, to relax, and to find out what I wanted out of life. Being fifty-eight hit home a few times, but I was used to starting over. The virtual vagabond in me wouldn't quit.

Fun and Silly; It Does a Body Good

This is great, I thought. *A course online that sounds like a lot of fun.*

Dressing Your Truth by Carol Tuttle teaches you to discover your own type of beauty, and that anyone's body shape can look amazing in the right clothes, colors, and accessories. Through this course, I found a part of me that was fun and silly, a side I was always afraid to show. I learned to lighten up. Why do I tell you this? Because I still had weight issues and still struggled in other areas like finances and relationships. So I took the intro course, which was free, and liked it so much that I continued with it.

What happened was amazing. I didn't change anything; I just rearranged my outer appearance. I found out I was a type-one woman with an upward, light, and spontaneous kind of energy. Instead of wearing a lot of black, which I thought made me look thinner, I chose bright colors and bold accessories. It was out of character for me. I changed the color of my hair and got a new style. Wow! The responses I got were so positive, it made me feel wonderful. All I was doing was bringing out my authentic self, the one that was hidden for so long. The funniest thing is that when I dated, the guys made comments about loving my "look," and specifically my red hair. *Interesting.*

Back to Kushi, in a Good Way

I had always wanted to do volunteer work of some sort, but working in retail and the constant schedule changes made it impossible. Not having that pressure anymore, I was able to try something different. I headed back to the Kushi Institute.

It was my home away from home, and I felt good being there. It was a win-win situation. They were looking for volunteers, so the timing was perfect.

The hours, even as a volunteer were long, but I didn't mind them at all. It was busy and fun working beside some of the most amazing macrobiotic chefs. People came there for all sorts of reasons: to get healthy, to stay healthy, and to learn. On my days off, I sat in on lectures, absorbing everything I could. I walked through the mountains daily and was excited to find an entrance to the Appalachian Trail, a place I would go back to and walk as much as I could for the month I was there. I was sad to leave but happy to get home to my family. The staff wanted me to stay, but, let's face it; I had to find a paying job.

I was in Massachusetts for about a week when I got a call from my son saying that his dad, my ex-husband, had passed away. He was a big chain-smoker his whole life, so it wasn't a surprise to hear he had lung cancer.

Jeff and his dad never had a great father-son relationship, but this was still his dad. My daughter felt the same way. I was far away and hoped the kids would be OK. Hearing the news made me sad—sad that my kids didn't have the dad they deserved and even sadder that he had suffered in his last days.

Late one evening, when my shift was over, I decided to talk to Bill. There was a bench and a big tree on the side of the mountain, so I went there for some quiet time. I knew he could hear me. I knew he was near. I told him how angry I was and that he was a horrible person. I asked him why he had hurt his children for so many years when he could have helped them. Instead, he chose another path and forgot all about them. I was hurting, and I cried, and then I forgave him. It was a long and emotional conversation.

The following December, I had a small gathering at my house, and a medium came to give us readings. She said my husband was there, and he was sorry. She said he heard me and knows I tried to forgive him that day on the mountain. I had no doubt.

I began looking back on what I had learned, with certifications in many things, and wondering what I could do with all of them. Meditation became a daily ritual once again. I began going back to my ministry by actively studying a *Course in Miracles*, and it renewed my faith and belief in how important forgiveness was. I began forgiving, first myself, and then others.

True forgiveness is when you can say...thank you for that experience.
—Oprah Winfrey

It's Forgiveness

Loving someone is not nearly as difficult as forgiving someone, but, forgiveness, I think, is the answer. To forgive is to be free, free to love, free to be yourself.

Forgiving another is one of the hardest things to do. Nobody likes to do it because it takes work, and it makes you feel vulnerable. It also gives you a choice because you can't be judgmental or upset. As I said before, it's never about the other person; it's only about you, so that you can move on.

When we forgive, we open our hearts. When we open our hearts, we begin to change and get rid of any fears that we may be harboring. Fear and love can never occupy the same heart. The hardest part of forgiveness, for me, was to forgive myself. It was much easier to forgive others because I always blamed myself for situations. I thought it was the righteous thing to do. How misguided I was.

Forgiveness Meditation

Please relax; just get comfortable. You may want to lie down on a bed or stretch out on a chair. Begin breathing slowly and gently, in and out, as you close your eyes. As you continue your breathing, imagine a beautiful circle of white light entering your heart. Now think of someone you'd like to forgive or that you need forgiveness from.

See this person, and imagine him or her growing small, until he or she rests gently in the palm of your hand. In your mind's eye, take this person and put him or her into your heart, breathing ever so gently. You can say, "I forgive you," if you like, but it doesn't matter. You don't need to say anything. Stay with that person for a moment.

If there's anyone else you would like to bring into your heart of forgiveness, you may do it now. You can fit many in there, so don't worry about overcrowding.

When you're done, take another deep breath in, and, when you breathe out, gently hold out your hand with the person or persons in it and softly blow their energies into the air. When ready, you can open your eyes.

I do this meditation often, and it's amazing how powerful and simple it is. There was a coworker I had known for years, and we hadn't spoken in a long time. The morning after I did this meditation, he came over to my desk and asked me if he could give me a hug. I was quite impressed to say the least. I'm sure you will be too.

When I was willing to let go of what I wanted, I realized what was truly mine.

—Anita Moorjani
author, speaker

Chapter 17

One Step at a Time

When I stopped looking to dictate everything outside of me to run the course of my life, I began to take control of me. I knew instinctively that I had all I needed inside of me. The answers were there; they always were.

I became a bit selfish in that I started caring about me more than others. I learned to say no. Although I listened and respected others' opinions, it was me whom I trusted. It was that inner being that always knew best and has always been there for me.

All I had to do was pay attention and listen to that inner voice. When I did that, I began to take it easy on myself.

Trying to get back in the workforce after a year away was not easy. I had some forty years of experience behind me in so many different things, but it didn't matter. I tried my hand at a few things, like short-order cook and taxi driver to name a few, and finally settled for a position at a large drugstore chain.

The job, as it was explained to me, sounded promising. The actual job was not. I tried to justify being there by saying that I was helping senior citizens who lived in the area. The truth is, I was helping to dispense drugs, and plenty of them, to hundreds of people. It was ironic, knowing how I felt about pharmaceutical companies. Here I was, handing out heavy-duty prescriptions to unsuspecting seniors every single day.

As much as I liked the people I worked with, I knew I couldn't stay. After nine months, I had to walk away. That gnawing feeling in my gut told me it was time to go.

We all have the power within us to heal.

There will always be stuff coming up; that's

the nature of being alive. No matter what

your challenges are, health issues, money,

relationships, you can find the answers by

looking within and paying attention.

Your Body Will Speak to You;

Your Heart Will Heal You

-Author unknown/WebQuotes

Happy Birthday

My Facebook Post, April 19, 2016

I'm not a huge fan of Facebook but felt compelled to share today. Some might say turning sixty is young, and they'd be right. Others might say sixty is old, and they'd be right. I see it as a beautiful journey that continues to evolve. For me, it's shedding the old beliefs of who I thought I should be, how I should behave, how I should look. It's taken me a lifetime to love and accept myself, even with all my flaws and imperfections. Now I wear them proudly. Life will never be perfect, but then it wasn't meant to be that way. Why are we here, if not to learn? Each person we meet is a lesson for us and, I believe, a teaching. We give and take from each other. My wish for you is this: that you realize that everything you'll ever want or need is inside of you. You already have it. Don't look for others to give you the answers. Value their opinions and just love them for who they are, faults and all. Most importantly, remember to "lighten up," and remember that "happy really is an inside job."

Just a Little Bit of Luck

By now, you know a bit about me. I tell you my story because I want you to know that I'm just like you. We might seem different on the outside, but inside, we are quite the same. I wonder who you are, what your story is, and how you came to be here today. We all have the power to change, and sometimes we just need some guidance. We don't need someone telling us what to do, just some encouragement and support. Oh, and a little bit of luck. A dear friend of mine is always saying, "You just need to have a little bit of luck." I get it.

There's no perfect here, and there never will be. Even though I try my best to eat clean, I still struggle with weight issues, and I still get scared, but that's OK. What's not OK is to be anything less than the happy, beautiful, and loving human being you were meant to be. You deserve to have the kind of love in your life that you want.

To quote Oprah, "What I know for sure" is that I wake up each day feeling grateful and blessed for everything that I have in my life, and knowing that it's all perfect just as it is. It just takes some of us a little longer to figure it out.

In reflection, the road will take me where it takes me. I travel with a backpack, one that used to carry heavy stones, but now it's filled with things like love, contentment, peace and compassion, integrity, and perseverance.

Each day of my life is a blessing, and, oh how I love the rain. Whenever a challenge pops up, I take a breath, step back and say to myself, "OK, Deb. What's going on here, and is it real, or is it just your perception of truth?"

If you look into a person's eyes, really look, you'll notice a connection. Your intuition will kick in, and you may see deep down into that person's soul. This is where you'll remember the loving truth of who you are, not the other person, but you, and you'll feel grateful. It was never about them anyway.

So, I decided to write this book, and to tell you the truth, it's frightening. If I listened to others' opinions (and these are good people who love and care about me), I would've written their book, not mine, and not yours. I want you to find the joy in your life, and I want you to find your voice, no matter how loud you roar, or how quietly you whisper. Be courageous, and be brave enough to live life the way you were meant to.

Today, I live my life as authentically as I can, and, with great passion, I look forward to what the next chapter brings. Like you, I am a never-ending work in progress who is always in awe to where my new adventure leads. My wish is that we, together, live in the knowing that we're all OK—no, better than OK—perfect, just the way we are.

Never again will I be distracted by a world of illusions. I shall live my life in harmony with my soul, and a longing to be inspired by nothing less than butterflies and rainbows.

DEBBIE MARIE LIPPI

This book was inspired, among other things, by my experience at the Institute for Integrative Nutrition, (IIN) where I received my training in Holistic Wellness and Health Coaching.

IIN invites students to deeply explore the things that are most nourishing to them. It's about eating wholesome foods and the idea that everything in life (health, career, relationships, spirituality) must always work in harmony, contributing to our inner and outer health.

Feel free to contact me about my personal experience at **debwithgrace@gmail.com**

MY Semi- BOOK LIST

Goddesses Never Age	Christiane Northrup
Dressing Your Truth	Carol Tuttle
A Return to Love	Marianne Williamson
I Need Your Love, is that True	Byron Katie
The Language of Letting Go	Melody Beattie
The China Study	T. Colin Campbell
Plant Intelligence	Stephen Buhner
Code of the Extraordinary Mind	Vishen Lakhiani
Your Body Never Lies	Michio Kushi
The Renaissance Soul	Margaret Lobenstine
The Untethered Soul	Michael A. Singer
Big Magic	Elizabeth Gilbert
You Are a Badass	Jen Sincero

Did you like my book?

I would love your review.

Please give me your honest feedback
on Amazon.

Connect with me on
www.debwithgrace.com

For info on workshops:
email me @
debwithgrace@gmail.com

NOTES

NOTES

NOTES

www.ingramcontent.com/pod-product-compliance
Lightning Source LLC
LaVergne TN
LVHW051416080426
835508LV00022B/3114